The Flesh Between Us

Crab Orchard Series in Poetry
OPEN COMPETITION AWARD

The Flesh Between Us

POEMS BY **TORY ADKISSON**

Crab Orchard Review &
Southern Illinois University Press
Carbondale

Southern Illinois University Press
www.siupress.com

24 23 22 21   4 3 2 1

Cover illustration: photo by Ruslan Gilmanshin of stone statue detail of
human hand (cropped). ADOBE STOCK (#242796927).

The Crab Orchard Series in Poetry is a joint publishing venture of
Southern Illinois University Press and *Crab Orchard Review*. This series has
been made possible by the generous support of the Office of the President
of Southern Illinois University and the Office of the Vice Chancellor for
Academic Affairs and Provost at Southern Illinois University Carbondale.

Editor of the Crab Orchard Series in Poetry: Allison Joseph
Judge for the 2020 Open Competition Award: Brian Turner
Jon Tribble, series founder and editor, 1998–2019

Library of Congress Cataloging-in-Publication Data
Names: Adkisson, Tory, 1987- author.
Title: The flesh between us / Tory Adkisson.
Description: Carbondale : Crab Orchard Review : Southern Illinois
   University Press, [2021] | Series: Crab Orchard series in poetry |
   "Open competition award." | Summary: "Intensely and unapologetically
   homoerotic in content and theme, this book explores the limits of sexual
   intimacy, familial intimacy, and the attachments we have to ourselves,
   arguing that our connections to each other may be lovely or painful,
   static or constantly shifting, but are, above all, unavoidable and
   necessary"— Provided by publisher.
Identifiers: LCCN 2020052836 (print) | LCCN 2020052837 (ebook) |
   ISBN 9780809338429 (paperback) | ISBN 9780809338436 (ebook)
Subjects: LCGFT: Poetry.
Classification: LCC PS3601.D547 F58 2021 (print) | LCC PS3601.D547
   (ebook) | DDC 811/.6--dc23
LC record available at https://lccn.loc.gov/2020052836
LC ebook record available at https://lccn.loc.gov/2020052837

Printed on recycled paper ♻

CONTENTS

The Flesh Between Us

SELF-PORTRAIT WITH MY EIDOLON

All I know is how to shiver.
I was born in rain and continue to live there.
I want to believe when you say
it's warm and I can't feel it. Belief is a word that rests
cold and heavy on my tongue.
If, someday, it evaporates, I will relinquish
time as just another figure to measure
my existence along with my height, weight, waist,
and dick size. Men are very particular
about these things. When the seasons change
so do I, signaling you with a cuttlefish's
war paint, the undulation of color on my skin
hypnotizing you into a long sleep
you might never wake up from. I'm not so cruel.
Some days I want to know your cloudless
world, the soft sighs in every stanza of your palms.
Some days I want to wrestle
an angel to the ground just so he can know
its flavor. I see in you a childhood
full of dust devils, a country with my name.
I see in you a place to mouth
dumb questions to a god that doesn't have
words enough to answer.

THE GARDEN

after James Merrill

Dream the dream called dirty
laundry & dress me
as you like: knee-high

stockings of a call girl, feathered hair
of an Indian boy pulling
arrows, his bow strung.

Remember: point to shoot.
Tonight, I pull your body
taut from the quiver, watch it fall

apart in lost fletchings. Lilacs
sprout from the small of a statue's
back as it bends away from us,

grasping for the hand of a friend
whose body, once handsomely
defined, has worn smooth & round

as a cat's eye. The air around us
condenses into locusts: a whole
life spent digging for eggplants

& daikon to make a stew.
I should've mined the vegetables
from my body, realized

I have a turnip for a tongue.

ANECDOTE OF THE PIG

Do you still believe myths
can save you? Foolish creature.
Let me be clear: every version of the story
ends with you being slaughtered.
I am not sorry to share this.
In life, as in death, we cannot be too deliberate.
Don't turn your fleshy
ear away while I'm speaking!
Ignore the metal hooks clinking together
like ice in the freezer, the unseen
saw grinding through snout gristle.
You can raise a sliver of someone
else's flesh to whatever god you
worship, just don't expect me to grease
my teeth with anything else before the meal.
Now go to the kitchen where an exotic
woman waits to kiss your throat
open & touch her red nipple to the wound.
Neither of us remembers your human
name. At least we remember
you were human. Isn't that enough?

GNOSTIC AUBADE

In the morning, *say what is the beautiful*
thing that is broken? Say we do not sing
one song. The morning comes suddenly,
the light cutting across the door
like a blade, the sun is quick, opaque,
& white, within a cat's paw.
So say *let's sit awhile in a state of awe,*
let's tap on the glass until we hear
a heartbeat or the beating of wings—
& look, there's a damselfly circling
the empty space, her eyes
compound, compound, compound: *you are*
just one of many copies. The morning
is when we pray & drink coffee
& invent a new language consisting
mostly of warbles. Your hand wakes.
Remember forgetting to lock the door?
So find the stranger in your bed.
His body isn't as foreign or rotten
as you think. Say *yes, I know how*
he got here—how all of us got here—
even though you don't. You couldn't.

THE FAUN

Some nights it came
with long, unmanageable hair
on staggered footfalls,

its breath spiked with whiskey,
a pair of ravenous hands
forever willing to bless my neck

and thighs with bruises
shaped like cat's eyes. Its hands
didn't know the meaning of kindness—

it would watch me sleep for hours
before peeling back the rind
from my softest parts to pierce them

with its tongue, masturbating me
until it grew so titillated its tall
horns scraped bits of stucco off the ceiling.

Only then could I draw its thistle
flute into the smallness of my mouth
and play the only song I knew

that would make it go away,
a shrill whistle like an animal call,
the sound of one heart closing as another

opens, drawing darkness in
with each beat. It was like that:
a cruel song, but sweet.

SPRING IN PARADISE

You are the one who whispered
of butterflies. Now all I can see

is their red irises, their wings
thin as apple slices, the branches of my trachea

snaking down my stoma, where
the soft light flutters in a string

of silvery feathers. You are the butterfly,
curled proboscis quizzically

scrounging for the sweet scent
of decay. In awe, I wonder *where are the flowers*

& *the boy who held them?* His veiny feet
covered in asphodel, the doorknob to his room

subsumed by ivy & sycamore leaves.
I felt you leaving even before you left, & still

the children sowed dandelions in sawdust,
whispered to the maple & elm

how their three-points beckon toward
divinity. We yellow in autumn

with the rest of the world. Return his petals
if you can't return his body. I wanted to know

your voice once, but after you left
I never wanted to know it again.

Now you've come back with *I love
you*, pricking my skin like a wasp.

My viscera remain calcified & solid.
You'll be waiting a long time

before I tell you anything like *love*,
before I utter even a single syllable.

You'll wait until your rigorous hands
have receded into twilight
& my hollowness with them,
for the cocoons of my eyes to lash

open: a pair of diaphanous
wings unfolding at their center.

CALIFORNIA

Take the highway through my body. Never doubt the route. The sky's
so big out here you could kiss a cloud if you realigned your vertebrae.
Downward dog. Eye of the needle. Sycamores rise unheeded, simulacra
for the bodies of the men I've known, ribbed, knuckled, tasted. Like
leaves, their tender frottage. Try memorizing mountain roads, the
long way up through the canyons. Carry a compass & flashlight if
you're in need of direction. I'm all journey, no destination, no secret
spot for perfect surf. Just treetops crowding the horizon. Drive as
fast or slow as you want. I'm steep on the sides, your back is stippled
with freckles. That shadow out in the water might be a whale, might
not. Whatever you want, I'm your imagination.

ODE TO SNEAKERS

Cleveland, Ohio

arranged in a pile, stinking like wildflowers,
used gym socks protruding

from their mouths like stamen.
Why is the stink of bacteria so alluring to me?

The accumulation of single cells in a dark,
damp sole, the minutiae of Adidas, Chucks,

& Nikes lying on the floor
with mute tongues. This is my secret

that stops being a secret
when I write it. There are four guys

living here, around twenty or twenty-five pairs
between them. Upstairs I hear them snoring,

masturbating, watching old war movies
while I lean low & lift a shoe to my nose

to inhale its bitter acid. I'm breathing in
a chronicle of the day's many male

labors—running track, basketball, P90X—
with closed eyes, aware that this metonymy

can't draw me to a field, or us any
closer, than *taste* or *touch* might.

It's too dark. Too difficult to grasp anything beyond
myself—& even then, being invisible is exciting.

Just listening is exciting. Above me
thunder rolls, mattresses squeak, bombs

are going off. Down here, I'm facedown in the chasm
between shame & denial, my erection

a bridge to a better, more sensual world.

TO BE LOVED

We dipped our fingers in milk
so the cats would love us.
To keep their love, we braided
the bones of three mice
in our hair, used one of their
skulls for a thimble. It's a myth
we used to make violin
strings from cat guts. The noun
is crucial. We made the strings
from *catgut*, the intestines
of sheep or hogs, which we found
less precious. Less worthy of our love.
It's such a delicate thing—
fleshy-tailed, scabbed, mottled.
We drink our milk & breathe
heavily so the cats know where
it's gone. They blade our throats
to get at it, to lap it up, & we
let them. *We love them.*
We wish we too could drink.

FIGURE STUDY

once I was an apprentice
or maybe just

a jar in the kiln
my lips worked over by his hands

my hands working
the flat handles of his ribs

each second flattened
against my palms as I pressed them

deeper & deeper into the clay
expecting his hands to leave

trenches in my stomach
or a concave ghost of his tongue

against my shoulder
matching his toothmarks

it was too much sometimes
making war in that bottle

& not love
never love

against the terrible porous
sulk of our enamel

he'd eventually turn to sketching
portraits of me instead

portrait after portrait
I sketched of myself

the artist with red eyes
& a hilt with no blade

we wanted to feel mysterious
but drawing didn't make us

feel any more mysterious
than we already were to each other

than clay is to the hands
that shape it

than paper is to the pencil
tracing rough memories

on its white lotuslike flesh
he said once & only once

don't get attached
don't fall in love with me

which I've said & resaid
again & again to those few boys

that find themselves lying beside me
like carafes hemorrhaging

liquid from cracks in their bases
how I want to tell them

that I lied that it was possible
the instant a man's lips

circled my own
for the very first time

in an O that dissolved
quick as a ring of smoke

to love a man & not fear
the pebble of his body rippling

through the shallow pool of mine
how I want to tell them

everything changed when I closed
my eyes & nothing happened

PORTRAIT OF MY MOTHER AS PENELOPE

My father told stories my mother
told better.

When he left, she
read *The Odyssey* to me.

I learned about heroic similes
& epic flaws. But my knowledge bank

was frail—my father broke in again
& again to steal the memories I had of him

that still held value. In his absence
she sat weaving & unweaving

the predictable pattern of his story.
I tried my hand at the loom

but found my fingers too clumsy.
She asked me to comb her hair.

As we grew older, we took swigs
of ouzo until it lit our throats on fire.

All the while, he shipped from shore to shore,
from Circe & Calypso,

while she kept her nails & thread
to the wheel,

spinning his praises
as long as she could, until the fabric

ran out & our dream ended
& finally my father returned home,

dressed as a beggar,
only that was who he was—

it wasn't a disguise.

ANECDOTE OF THE RABBIT

It shed its body the moment its breath
rattled beneath our undercarriage.
Mom was driving—
it was a warm desert night & she was speeding
as usual. We didn't know what had bolted
like an arrow from the margins of the road
until we saw a few tufts of fur hovering
in air, their descent so slow
it looked deliberate. Mom didn't
turn her head, didn't close her eyes,
blotched purple & red like crushed tulips,
as her many-ringed fingers righted the steering wheel.

After all, it was summer. No time for grieving.
Later, barbecuing, she'd daub
chicken thighs & pork shoulders
with marinade like a ceramicist
applying glaze. We'd sit at the table,
waiting for her to arrange meat & vegetables
on plates, setting them before us.
We didn't acknowledge
anything: what happened after we hit the rabbit
was fiction: the stories we tell ourselves
over & over to keep the guilt in our bodies
from stirring, not even for a minute.

DUENDE

The dark song, the churl, the way

you sing it, the way we fuck
        at twilight. You stayed up

late to see the harbor gray, waited
        for the sun to rake the sea

apart in several elongated shards.
        In your briefs you prayed

to me, to my knees, prayed for release
        but I washed my hands

of it, of you, of all these waves
        meticulously pulled under the hull

of your boat. The night spread
        before us in fragments: you, me, glass,

ring, cock—& this perception
        seemed natural. Scrotum, sock. You spread

my legs apart, kissed a white
        spot on my bare thigh for clarity

or direction. My body was never
        prophecy the way you saw it—

the hair between my legs could never
        tell you what door to open. The point

of asking is not to receive an answer
   but to make your own anxieties known

with each sea-elephantine
   groan—For love? For pleasure?

Who knows? Only the breath you carry
   & the blood in your exsanguination jar

divine much truth anymore.
   Beyond your molecular composition

what else is there to say? I've felt
   the ridges of your dark vessel, its prow

a bullet tearing through a bleak
   & tender muscle—& never once did you

direct it at me, as if to suggest *it's you*
   I will murder. No. Even now, it slides

down the Styx with remarkable
   pomp, a single ravenous wing

breaking back through the keel.

SUMMER IN PARADISE

There is the sudden sting of orchids
on my path. There is a bed of orchids

instead of your body. I crawl into it, furtive.
When I do I furrow.

There is the clean song
each finch flinches——& a hard

shade of brown coating
your irises. There is only so much

breath in my body, only
so much of it you can steal. I'd give it

willingly, but that's not the point,
is it? There is this moon on my lap.

This convocation of crows echoing off
the sides of cliffs. Bats boomeranging

back to their caves. Mayflies mating.
These are my hands, a gamble of roses

carded out, suit-side down.
(What to play, what to play.)

That is my obedience lining
the soft meat of your throat.

There it is, an ex-
action, staccato.

HOMOSEXUALITY

Desire, I drape over my chest
so you know what flag I bear,
what nation I want to land on
when the rescue workers
& newscasters have pulled me
from the dark, allowing me to
rinse my foliate feathers, shed
my oily skin—& with wings
steeped in fire, they won't be able
to look at me—the light would burn
pinholes in their pupils—
& what they will ask as they kneel
is *How long does the bridge run
in your heart, how deliberately
dark is the birdcage?* I will give them
an answer, & after they've kissed
my feet, I will give them a pair
of sunglasses, so when I sit down
to eat they'll be able to see clear
through my throat to the window
behind it & wait their turn to
bring a knife & fork to the table.

LUSUS NATURAE

Between the sheets, it's the same in the forest:
thriving on quiet moments of violence,

     where we have the same tugged-on
     hair, drink from the same empty stream.

Hunt, rut, hunt. Against these mottled logs
we loom like giants, snail shells jutting

     from the bark like houses built into a cliff.
     I whisper. O how I want it, the tickle

in my shorts. The *little death* that presages
my inevitable resurrection. Waterfalls are only

     arresting for so long. *Pin a man to moss*
     and what does he learn? You, how to grow.

Me, how to worm. Green weather brings
ants from the anthill, their tiny bites tiny nicks

     of love. Or I want them to be. Without our flesh
     they'd continue their march, just as the forest

is forever full of animals we still haven't seen.
The fox I thought I saw bleeding past my nipples

     wasn't a fox. It was a fern. A red fern. A fern on fire.

SOMEWHERE BETWEEN MEMORY

A school of minnows slip
through my fingers. Their bodies

flint. The past winnows into a procession
of a million small, conscious minds,

each a measurable part, a whole
unto itself. This is the tragic

magic of dreaming, of reaching
for a hand & always darker for it.

Some life filters through the cracks
like straw. My palms are full of empty water.

The psalms can't reach them.
Feel their sweat & there is no answer

save a whisper edging into the soft
room of the throat; more real, it seems,

than swimming through the waves
lapping at the shore of each occurrence.

But history & its variant currents: fins stalk
close behind me, enigmatic, so I close

my eyes, hold the air in my mouth
as long as the water holds me on its tongue.

Time & its longing shatter like tiny
bits of shell. Look how faint the marks are.

How little they ripple. Sometimes.

ANECDOTE OF THE OSPREY

        Babies plummet
like stones from their mother's

      basket, barely alive, their shells
shellacked & cast aside to humble

them in the aether. There is no time to be young.

      She's decided they should learn
a thing or two about the clouds

fanning out in hydra's-heads,
       the gilt apparatus of thunder.

The wind & mother
      blend into a single susurrus.

        Then the *snap* of her
talons, open like switchblades.

Her duty is not to her children,
      but to nature—she is a servant,

      splitting the air into roiling
         shards. Light strikes her babies' heads

in a fistful of matches. That's what's so harrowing

       & delicate about a bird's
first flight: we almost lose

sight of Icarus—his perilous

    decline—before we realize

        she, too, could be falling

    where there are no hands

willing to catch her.

TAMING EROS

a bouquet of arrows
for your thighs. for your heart,

a bouquet of matches.
strike each head against

your head. get them to flint. not
another way of talking, but a better

way to see mortality. as a blessing.
stop short of flight—it won't get you

very far; instead cull a bouquet
of crimson, a bouquet of cinnabar,

finally sulfur. let the loose
feathers dart off, one at a time. then

make a pillow, go to sleep,
learn to be human, dream.

learn desire, that which you cannot have:
a quiver of throats, a quivering tongue.

WITHOUT BRAINS OR BACKBONE

Questions come & go like bees
    in their hive: we're afraid to ask,
so we lick the pollen from their thoraxes

instead, trying to discern direction
    by taste alone when we should be
dancing. Or we study the world

as moths do, from a distance,
    until a flame appears & draws us

closer, then closer, to self-
    immolation. Life burns chasing
hard truths, a vanity we afford

ourselves by virtue of speaking it.
    Imperfectly, we try to tell each other
secrets while no one else watches,

compound eyes glued
    to their screens. The knowledge
we inherit emerges in stages:

larval, pupal, molting forever
    into new shapes until the juvenile
wings have fallen

off, replaced by the ptero
    -stigma of adulthood. Some of us
skip more easily to exoskeletons

of suits & ties. Beyond the nymph
	stage, mandibles suspended in a permanent
state of awe. (They crave so much & can't

even chew paper!) Yes, it hurts
	to grow, to learn the mechanism
of a new body, but we're better knowing

the ache of that wonder, the sting
	jutting through the abdomen.
Someday the raqiya of the nest will

collapse, & we'll need the scraps
	to build a new colony, one
where I can be your queen (or king),

& you can help propagate a new
	species of mystery: hybrid forms
born to be sentient & buzzing.

X & Y

We are always an arm's-
          length from each other.
                    As elephants

to ivory. More bones
          than we know: twisted
                    jackal teeth, toucan

calami, diamondback
          rattles. Embellishment
                    is our specialty.

We work our oars
          in opposite directions.
                    We anchor the world.

We are the sound of broken
          windshields, trampled
                    teakettles. We are brittle,

we are broken. We are the suburbs;
          old, war-torn Europe.
                    Enough white on our flags

for the rest of the world.
          We are unknown
                    even to each other.

We are the only remaining
          coordinates on the map.
                    Not the color of rust.

But red. Not blood,
       or authority, or
              authorship.

Closed eyelids, yes.
       The exact tincture
       of burn.

THE THRONE

When the earth swallows
stars in its throat, cicadas are short
to follow. A leash of foxes
huddle around a pool of muddy water
like a circle of flame.
Dusk falls in particles of silent
precipitation on the heads of stags
who no longer remember
they used to be human. Their names fade
further into the distance with each
cleft of skull against skull, with each
branch of gnarled wisteria their hooves
bend and twist into the shape
of a makeshift throne.
A god comes staggering out of the darkness,
oozing wine from his wrists
as he bleats and bleats for help.
Only the owls listen, which he—
in his delirium—mistakes
for a choir of angels. They descend
with the finality of a shroud,
leaving shafts of broken arrows in their wake,
and bits of undigested bone
arranged in the shape of a crown
for the next god
that comes to take his place.

CORONATION

The oak whispers *give in*,
give in through its brambles, tugging
at the black twine of your hair,
writhing like Medusa's weave
pulled loose—a sudden throng of snakes
pulsing in the mud. How goes your own
hectic slither? Because you hunt for rabbits,
grouses, deer, & quail, for the queer
cherries of their eyes macerating
the dark, I know your taste is for
more than blood. You have a tongue
for ribs & ankles, enough spines to lick
an owl's head clean of feathers.
Kestrels flinch in the branches & beg
tinder the trunks. You wonder
if they wander the damp hollow
of your belly for their new home, if they know
it's safer to be within you than without.
Every night, I call back to the broken
stones where our union began.
Where you took on my bondage.
Where, howling over my belly, the spruce
& pine needles sketched a red
crown around your temples. Remember,
in these woods you learned my speech
by imitating the white vowels
of the moon. But only *my* mouth—
a crater indifferent to affection—
can pull voices from the trees,
their echoes & eyeless sockets.

PORTRAIT OF MY MOTHER AS DEMETER

She bends to the quiet thought
        of hunger, how best

to manage it. She lifts a cornstalk
        from her purse & sticks it

in my ear. *There is still more*
        work to be done. I haven't

learned how to care for her yet,
        how like an animal

she begs to be cleaned when
        she can still clean herself.

How intimately I relate to that
        on a human level.

Yet she's never been human.
        To me, she's always been

mother. Some mornings she still
        remembers arranging

boxes of cereal so I could choose
        my own capricious flavors.

It changed every day. So much depends
        upon skim milk & slivers

of bananas. So much depends upon
        a spoonful of blueberries

in each bowl. She insists we still
        depend on each other, that

I was the baby she tried to bake
        immortal in the fire.

I've always known she could
        chuck me in the oven

if she wanted, just to remind me
        how little wit is worth,

how easily life burns away
        the wax on your feet, the dry

pine of your hair. She probably
        placed me on the coals

thinking *ritual is a volatile act*,
        convinced the skin was a faith

worth returning to—& melting
        the fat, watching it liquefy

in the pot, meant more to her
        than just hunger, as if watching it

harden could solve the problem
        of love, of memory, of grief.

CICADAS

Their bodies arranged in the shape
of an ankh. Suddenly summer
is ending. I found another lying
silent in an empty plastic bottle.
It was cessation. How else do you
describe the trees when they stop
their buzzing? When the wind no longer
shoots through their spiracles? I shake
the bottle to see if the husk will stay
attached. No, it falls off, a small
heap of ash. Autumn is coming.
Every few years it gets like this—
their sudden swarm, their ephemeral
departure. Food for hawks. The stuff
of haikus. Such a thing, too: black
bodice, lace wings, & red glittering eyes.
They still hold their power.
The ankh sweeps away. My toes,
bare in the mud, & half a pomegranate
in my hand. I save the rest for later.

YOUR ANIMAL HEART

Hidden in the woods—a mask
for Halloween, a mask

for winter. We slip into our holiday
frocks, never shedding a single

article or appendage. Soon
we grow, overgrow, tangled

& wild, weary & wistful—
fear holds a small knife to the tubes

of your throat. I'm powerless.
I can only save myself.

Please, love, don't swallow
your questions. Let's drink the forest

& forget the animals,
the brambles stuck infinitely

in their soles. Hawks are hawkish.
Eels squirm. You can't remember

the urge that brought us
together, or forget the urge

that's pulling you away: our ragged
arms, the sick, suckling meat

of our hearts. Before you discard
your mask, go & ruin the game

for all future players.
Don't break my body—break it free.

HOMOPHONE

When your bed is too well made
to be any kind of invitation, we spill
ourselves on the kitchen floor,
my hairy torso your mop, though
cleanliness is last on our minds—first
comes the music of the throat, percussive
bones, skin taut to the neck, the wood.
The liturgy comes with parishioners,
a circle of olive pits & cigarette
butts from the pew of your ashtray.
The cold tile holds a black mass, creasing
demonology down my back.
You say you desire me more than the sun
desires the moon. You recite Li Po,
describing the dense crescent
of my skull. The curdled milk
of my cuticles.
                But I am not the ghost
you think I am. I am flesh & you are
my fixation—penitent, & I hope, merciful.
You sing *wo ai ni*, tucked between my
thighs, the air thick with hair. You think
this is love, but it gets lost in translation.
I whisper what you really mean to say—
I harm you. I harm you. I harm you.

AUTUMN IN PARADISE

Below the skyline snaps
a branch, a fruit, an oblong

femur. The chlorophyll levels
drop. Leaves break; they are

brittle. Lice wriggle through the trunk
of the day. Peel back stars to reveal

radials in darker & darker shades:
fields striated with plumage & pelts.

Children play hopscotch
on lopsided patches of asphalt;

heaven folds over their heads like newspaper
when it rains. The bell rings & recess is over.

It gets worse in winter: your irises
saucer black to find what little

light there is left. This month
there is still enough of it to find

the beveled fruit, naked shoulders
with their studded freckles

& flash of puckered red, radiating
not from the sun, the moon, or the fire-

flies haloed in the garden, but from the seeds
in the sky. Dangerously, they scatter.

THE MEADOW

I took you into my mouth. Where my mouth took you

is anyone's guess. You fed me a single biscuit, placed

a wafer on my tongue & told me to swallow.

I was raised Jewish. I told you I didn't know the ritual,

didn't know what is gained or lost in this act of attrition.

We cannot build a community this way. Your body tightened

along its masculine edges. You wanted me to be

a perfect vessel when you entered, to graze something

pure & astonishing beyond my partitions: the gold

antler of a hind brushing past, the scrim of its tail. But perfection

only lasts as long as it takes to tug a thread of yarn

from your unspooling throat. Or as long as it takes the moon

to rise & the stags stirring in the field

to fall silent & jubilant beneath its glare.

ANECDOTE OF THE FOX

see her rove
through sycamores

see her rove
tail tufting out in a fan

of flames
see her cubs rove

through the woods
burning an arc

through the woods
like a wild waking eye

see her stalk them
distant & priestly

vixen she whispers
vixen she rises

behind the trees
a woman takes her place

see her loose hair
fall like a shadow

over her lucid skin
when a gunshot

shatters the icicle
silence she wanders

out on hands & knees
she wanders

toward the flickering
moon solemn

& bright see her dance
there like a struck candle

FIRST HARVEST

Watch how he lessens
his gait. The brim of his hat
tilts slightly, a halo

of salt encircling
his brow, just visible in the shadows.
I'm attracted to the metal

rivets of his tractor. It wallows in oil
before meticulously picking
through the cornfield, one

stalk at a time. I'm new to this
whole idea of harvesting.
The desert I love is full of needles

& no one ever picks them.
The moon's seasonal orange
has never been, for me, a mask

celebrating the coming
winter. Here the leaves change
color, wither,

& die. Nature reminds us, not too
subtly, that this is what we all do.
For now this boy will have to hold

my attention. I've watched him
change along with the weather,
his summer tank top

gilded with sweat. His spring
jersey, autumn wool & flannel.
Still the strain of work

persists like a flame. Still the sweat
persists, the crotch of his jeans
stretching thin, the stench

of manure & compost caked
into his boot heels. The exact point
of hunger, the soles

I must follow. Some nights
he's alien. Like the moon,
he doesn't notice me idly

paging through a book. Some nights
he doesn't notice he's the one
who's smiling.

SELF-PORTRAIT DURING A TORNADO SIGHTING

Through the window I see a murmuration
of starlings bat against the weathervane

like bullets of rain & feel my buzzing
thigh—texts & social media

tear across the great plains & rocky
mountain states, heralding news

of earthquakes in California.
My mother's messages are *worry, worry*—

paraphrased, my replies read *guilty, guilty.*
I type furiously: *i dont see the twister*

though I do, transfixed as the swirl
pummels trees in the distance, licking

its fists with every advance. The television
offers no advice—red, green, & yellow

flash over a map of Ohio
as if the state were a cuttlefish

mesmerizing its prey with a light show.
I am god-scared now, seeing the layers

of grit & shearing-magic too closely.
God is taking his drill to the earth.

My yarmulke will not protect me—
ducking-&-covered on a second-floor

apartment building—wearing a loose
helmet of fingers over that.

I'm down to a lone match flickering
in the tar-dark, listening to the trauma

in the tornado sirens' automatic bleating—
not for the cyclone, but for the birdless

quiet that follows.

WILDERNESS OF FLESH

I nuzzle the wheat
field of your armpit, whisper
how I like the fragrance,
sour as a rotted
onion.
       The wilderness
    of flesh we both
inhabit rests deep in the quarry
of your skull, in the scat
fertilizing your chest,

& the sound that pours from
the brook of your throat
swells like a magpie's
shriek, or a bullfrog
belching after
         home, & tonight—
      even if we flit in
& out of sleep like cardinals
winding through an ash
grove—our separate skins

will dissolve in the dark
musk of our mutual tug

& pull, our bodies nothing
less than a stick & stone
set to flint.

POSTMORTEM AUBADE

The scalpel carves out
a sliver of bone where the humerus
hollows into the shoulder
blade. Be careful removing
soft tissue—the cartilage & keel,
the lungs branching like cedars
down the trunk of the sternum.
When you pull the brain out, wrench it
softly so the stem, like an umbilical
cord, comes with it. Remove
one wing, then the other. Splay them
on the table & take notes on proportion, on arc—
how crowlike they are, how they seem
capable of flight in only the most dire
circumstances. The only conclusion
you can draw at this time is the cause
of death was exposure. When you're finished
allowing your gloves to plummet
from your hands like robin's
eggs, don't hesitate to break
the halo: another word for wish
-bone, another word for *worry*.

ECHOLALIA

Lay me in the ash. Ask
the asp if it knows

which way is home.

*Isn't it in your human
heart?* it might whisper

earless, poison

-pocked. What can
you tell a thing that

cannot hear how

we found our

ears pressed together,
how we reneged

when the kernels we begged

popped white as country

stars, as the egg

folded in the asp's un
-answerable curls.

How can you lay
down with me

if you can't think of any

-more doomed questions?

PORTRAIT OF MY FATHER AS THE TROJAN HORSE

Say *father, father* & listen for war. Stay
quiet and listen for a drum-

beat, the same as the heart of war.
The breath of men is a reckless sound

that splinters in the throat. Dad drinks
a little then a little more, and I wait and I wait.

When the Greeks leave they leave their shadows
burned into the walls, their ships

hurtling away from the coast
like a wake of vultures toward another

carcass that must be pillaged.
All it took to sack the city of Troy

was letting the wrong horse into its stables.
And me? I was the poor fool who listened

against the slats of his wooden
flank for a sound like love

and always let him in.

ANECDOTE OF THE SWAN

its head deep in your wetness
the way you know the body, slick

necked, a loose string of pearls,
a bill that folds your legs neatly

open like two slices of bread
all he wants he wants: a wing-

shaped bruise on your collar
bone or a collar around your throat

in place of the halo you wore
the night you met him

what you gave him you give
him, a morsel of tongue

you know will be fine and still
like an olive pit like the heart

of a lamb eager to be eaten
you never shiver at the fear

whipping through your hair
instead reciting your mantra

whatever will be will recede
into your rearview mirror

he follows you undeterred
unable to leave you even in the palace

of your womb which he insists
has room for even his most exalted

form, the shape of a bird you've never
been more or less eager to see

HORNETS

Their nests waffle in the breeze
like paper lanterns.

They threaten, they quiver. Our brains
float the same way in our cerebral

fluid. How can the air be anything
other than a curious spark?

Tell me the trees are brainstems
to invisible spines,

& the cardinals departing
their branches disappear into the dusk

like the names of old lovers,
the Japanese word for *contentment*,

because we're eager to lose them.
Forget my asthma & *miasma*,

forget your belligerent knuckles.
We watch the synapses snap

as each of the nests descends
in a volatile hail. We can't account

for the stale yellow of their dead.
So we don't.

What can we do but keep the sting of death
fresh on our tongues?

SCARECROWS

They are epitome at the end, their flayed skins
somehow able to move in tandem with the wind.
Their faint auscultations are just the rootings
of a fox that found them huddled together
after falling from their stakes. It tongues their remains.
Its tail divides until there are nine of them teeming
with a tiny flame. Before the fox chews off their fingers,
a passing buzz-worm's rattle scares it away.
Do these scarecrows epitomize the end? They still smile
around the ears, knowing they are destined to fall again,
just as Prometheus accepts the hawk into his liver
& the liver returns each day. At last the farmer sets them upright
so they can wave *hello, hello,* to their friends eyeing the sky
as they spread their atramental wings, too hesitant to fly.

WINTER IN PARADISE

Snow falls half as much
as it did when we were

younger. All the conifers
pine for more hours, spitting

threats from their ever
-green tongues. Flies

flock to them before
they freeze. Owls rest

heavy in the hand. How many
apples fell during harvest?

No one can tell. They've with
-drawn into caves along with

the many names we gave
the Earth: *terra firma, terra*

incognita, terra pericolosa.
Our feet scatter bullet holes

in the snow's white flesh. We still
don't know what to call this

place. We shrink & flail in
the dusk, chop the trees up

for kindling. The fire will rise
someday. We'll see the sun.

SORT SOL

When the birds form a chain

they change like the clouds change.
But the clouds only grow

darker. Wings

grow bigger & bigger
& more numerous. The way a field settles

beneath the sun's lazy gaze, slowly
drifting west toward a future

in which every horizon's

a departure. The way our hair is

growing into a demon with a tawny
head & umber tongue
can be scary.

Don't lose that fear, that fear of

breathlessness in the air. It will only
build your resolve.

Today the birds are charming, a vestigial

linkage, their shadows swarming over
the top of my head, my feet hurrying

below like a pair of stallions
caught in a flash flood we had

no warning of, because even if we did,

we wouldn't have wanted to hear it.

THE ORCHARD KEEPER

I know his body by the sound of his hands
working their way through brambles.

By the orchard where his spirit was spit on
& sharpened. His teeth cusped down

on my shoulder until it broke autumn-red
beneath the moon's slow flood

back when I thought bleeding was romantic.
We spent hours out there, rutting

in the mud, his hand pressed against my chest
like a talisman, stirring something

inside me, something to make me forget
how I'd never seen fireflies before—or felt love.

How everything I did was pretend.
Cautiously, I told him how little I knew

of what we were doing. How deep I felt
his hand scrape for apples I didn't carry.

The fireflies beaconing along the ground
lit up the slack nooses of his eyes.

I searched desperately for a hand
I could hold on to or follow. Surely

he could see my eyes, tied in sheepshanks,
couldn't bear his weight without failing.

ADAM'S APPLE

Think about the sin
you've swallowed, history
lodged in your throat.

Think about the pain
of eating fruit. How the origami
of your body can still split me

like a cantaloupe, or cut
my lip, or clip itself to me
like the paper I forget

to remember you are.
I'd welcome your blood's
matriculation into my throat

& feel the gnawed-on core
regain its shape as a sacrament
on my tongue. Its surprising pique

& density—you know the spade
of my mouth, the taste of pears,
their papery flesh. Some sensations

never lose their shape.
Just as the kink of your tongue
will always be like a word

of prayer against my palate.

DOUBTING THE GODS

Their voices saturate my body,
its dark a fault of theirs. Shrouded
in shale, I cling desperately
to the sides of mountains

while whole forests are devoured
by fires. *The wood has been
petrified.* They wink

from their thrones, sometimes coyly,
always with kohl eyes
through roof beams. If they write,

their ink is in the bats careening
through the stars, or the dense
flood of hawks gutting the pocked

cave of the skull. Each bird
a litany on a wire.
The moon is their movie theater.
If they do exist, they must roam

among dandelions & tiger lilies, making them
roar. They must perforate

every moment of our existence
the way an attic howls
above the house. They should have nothing to do

with love. In every pool of light,
they stagger & steal beneath the surface,

doling out a single fin
to keep us enthralled. When we happen
upon them, we can't help but fear

& feel drawn to the flutter
in their witness. We can't help
but utter *receive my salt, receive me.*

Perhaps they will.
Perhaps they nest in the center
of the wake like rafts of loons.

Perhaps if we ask politely
they will take us—
but only if we do not doubt
their power. We must allow them

to drown us & trust it will not be empirical
the way water fills our lungs

wholly, how their tentacles blacken
our already sable tongues.

ORIENTALISM

Through your navel, the sound
of the ocean opens, a cave's convex

darkness. Inside, a world
of Hokusai prints, octopuses

sprawled suggestively on the rocks.
Now we are both stars in each other's

wet dream. Shake the salt
from your hair, flip off the camera.

Whatever comes naturally.
I'm fine just fishing with a pair

of rough-cut hands, the delicious
gonads of sea urchins. All the better

for future stars of the Pacific
Theater, no longer encumbered

by war, its garish sound effects.
Blood. Now is a time for romance,

comedy, maybe even a *little*
catharsis. Or a story set to bamboo

flute about a Chinese man, dressed
as a woman, stabbing himself to ease

his anguish, for loving the sort of white
man who lusts only after travel,

who goes home to Europe promising
to return, when he is really saying

these are the roles we were born to play.
It's a pure sacrifice, playing them.

SELF-PORTRAIT AS A BUTOH DANCER

My feet patter—like rain, they
        stain each plot

of asphalt I clop over, shrieking
        like a kettle.

Peek behind the rice-cream
        makeup & break the illusion

if you must. Just don't deny my right
        to dance with limbs stiff

as a petrified forest. (I paint
        my tongue with squid ink.)

I jerk & prance & take this
        shroud on, genitals tucked

away, everything human about me
        concealed, hoping

Death will mistake me for one
        of its own & pass over me.

Behind the dark slip & crane-
        flecked kimono, I am only a young

man taking one more step in a series
        of steps, improvising not the howl

that pours from my cracked mouth
       like a darkness, but the fragile

contortion of my face: the ghoulish
       grimace, eyebrows penciled

high, the sweep of hair loosened like tulips
       hanging from a broken planter.

Though there's virtue
       in movement, sometimes

I'd like to lie still—not dead
       exactly, but naked

like a doll whose eyes
       close only when she tilts

her head forward, not when
       she sits up—or

dance like the ghost
       I know I will become, or

the ghost I've always wanted
       to be.

BAREBACK CARTOGRAPHY

It's as old as recorded history:
if a line wiggles, that's good.

The main skill is to keep from getting
lost, the result of low self-esteem

caused by the notion that only women get fucked.
Ask whether the best ones

always connect nowhere with nowhere,
the pungent scent stirred up

while we position ourselves
for better things, waiting for the sun

to crest and the season to open.
It took me so long to catch on

that secondary roads are preferred.
An unshaven back, an evident tan line,

or love handles are signs that one simply
doesn't care when every profile

reads fat femmes need not apply.
Still, I've learned to spot the good ones

on a map. We navigate mostly
by dead reckoning and deduction.

The more experienced scowl
and seem to be in a hurry.

Not me—for a passive observer
it all moves by boringly in a frame.

Proper lubrication and relaxation
helps prevent this problem.

AUBADE WITH TORTOISESHELL & OX

Our bones: the bread we break
to begin the conversation
about conversion. What stifles
my tongue is apotheosis.

You sand the edges of my femur.
We have to find our centrifugal point. Outside

the dialogues are material: hand-
kerchief, cufflinks, washboard, basin,
ridge & furrow. Writing is the interior
monologue pulled screaming

from the cellar. Too often we miss
cartilage & think only of the saw
& pulp: the sound, the sound
it cuts. Your wrists:

heavy as cups of water.
My skull: a window
impenetrable with night.
Pull away the curtain
& you'll see a soundstage—

men, with their cameras,
lean just inside the doorway.

There are a dozen microphones
bouqueted in my chest.

We love each other
like music: the pauses are telling.

Your breath could be
purposeful, could be a defect
in the recording. You play
operation like you mean it.
We're still busy poisoning
our organs. Wait it out—

you'll get your bladder back,
your heart, your lungs.
In the meantime, take my kneecaps;
they'll help you stand.

Take my metatarsals & hold me
a little longer. My mandible is brittle
so break it, break it until
a little truth falls out
with each tooth. Crack my spine

until the oracle whispers through the fissures.
Until the roar of the sea inside my throat

pours out of my mouth & into yours.

THOUGHT, BAREFOOT

—from a fragment by Sappho

The night: there is a blue thread
running from the sky's
nude seam. We watched   as the azul drooled
            down

the broken lip of every
fountain. The night before: you bruised
      your lip, cut

against the threshold
of your own teeth. You thought someone
      was there beyond   the stuffing

inside the boxes, thought you
discerned a flitting pair of moonless eyes,

pallid, an iota of waiting. You kept the string

tied to a callous lover, around his bare
torso. I placed a bit on my tongue,

handed you the bridle—
      crop-lashed at the hip.

Every breath, the clouds
crumbled like feta in the briny water

where the wingtips of little stone
cherubs were still visible.

Among the liquid dust.   Their music mute.

Tomorrow night: we are going
to trust where the arrow lands, & follow—

I thought: barefoot, because no matter
                                        how small the wound
the stone cuts into our heels,

                    there will still be a scar
          worth saving & you—a faith I need
                                        to break.

FALLOUT

Combing through the bones—marrow
pecked, a Portuguese
man-o'-war lies distended in the distance.
A film stretches across the horizon
shimmering at its edges. We've lived for
centuries under glass, how is it
that we're just now noticing? A boy will find
what remains of me speared through,
the shaft broken into splinters
beside a bag of popcorn full of unpopped
kernels. Every wisp of hair
will scintillate his neck, the texture
of reef broken between his exceptionally long toes.
The world is disintegrating into
a stream of red polyps. A patchwork of falcons
whip like a chain through the few
clouds we have left. *Eureka* they squawk.
Shut your fucking mouths a hog, far
beneath them, squeals.
I stretch a phantom hand toward
a cum-stained mirror, try to recall what it was like
when we loved ourselves.
Then I remember the bag of birdseed
I swallowed, my last words
now lost like plumage to the dark
hours of night. I've decided to become
a crow in the next life, because ravens are
too portentous and as a human
portentousness was my greatest flaw.
The birds disagree.
They say it was being human.

THE PROBLEM WITH WINGS

after Baudelaire

I am not trying to write

                        a poem about birds.

I am trying to write

                        a poem about that incandescent

weightlessness

                        we experience

when lying down

                        to sleep, to dream a false

dream in which I'm tying

                        a knot, not *the* knot—

not yet, not until I've earned

                        what little love

my life is worth.

                        I am trying to write

a poem in which no birds

                        appear, in which a cape

is all it takes to take

                        to the skies.

Superman, you think,

                        takes to the skies

trailed by a red cape,

                        & saves Lois Lane

from General Zod, Lex

                        Luthor, & Brainiac &

somehow she still doesn't see

                        he's just Clark Kent

without glasses, an alien

                        pantomiming back

what it means to be

human, to bleed that thin

strip of scarlet.

Maybe I can't write

a poem about flying

without considering

covert feathers stretching out

in radials, or the red

talons of raptors poised

to claim rabbits like tiny

wafers from green hands.

Maybe Superman

can't pretend to be a man without

pretending to be weak,

without stepping on his

glasses so he's un-

recognizable to the opposite

sex. That part

I'm reconciled to—I want men,

not women, to recognize me—

a *fagellah*. As a boy, my grandmother

would say—*look at those*

fagellahs prancing down the street,

though *fagellah* has nothing to do

with being a bundle of sticks,

a cocksucking heretic—

fagellah, a false cognate,

really means *bird*, really means

a small feathered thing

that flies when you throw it;

curves through the spokes

of the chest, through a gaggle

of handsome men walking,

their hands interlaced,
down Santa Monica pier.
Even if it's cliché, I want to be
a bird, unable to walk
the earth because my wings are
in the way.
Yet even with the stones
loose between my toes,
I've never been free, or any freer
than I am now, watching
the 'w' unfold between
my lover's shoulders, the
'i-n-g' breaking like silt
on my tongue.
The metamorphosis is definite
the moment I find love
wrapped like a knot around
his vowels. When he speaks
the creature
in my chest stirs
mightily & mad. *This is love.*
I'm tying the knot, writing
a letter to pin to his chest,
but the cupboard flaps open,
the creature flies away.
Again, I remember
this feeling isn't new.
The problem with wings
is knowing that
having them means
you can leave
whenever you want to—
& you will.

ACKNOWLEDGMENTS

I am grateful for the editors at the following publications, where many of the poems in this manuscript first appeared:

32 Poems: "Winter in Paradise"
The Adroit Journal: "Lusus Naturae," "Orientalism"
Anti-: "Sort Sol," "X & Y"
Barrow Street: "Adam's Apple"
Birmingham Review: "Autumn in Paradise"
Boston Review: "Without Brains or Backbone"
Boxcar Poetry Review: "Duende"
Cave Wall: "Anecdote of the Fox," "Anecdote of the Rabbit,"
    "Portrait of My Mother as Penelope"
The Collagist: "Gnostic Aubade"
Colorado Review: "Homosexuality"
Copper Nickel: "Coronation," "Spring in Paradise"
Crab Orchard Review: "Anecdote of the Osprey"
Crazyhorse: "Portrait of My Father as the Trojan Horse"
Cream City Review: "Somewhere Between Memory," "Figure
    Study"
CutBank: "Taming Eros"
Drunken Boat: "The Garden"
Failbetter: "Echolalia," "The Problem with Wings"
Grist: "The Meadow"
Jellyfish Magazine: "Your Animal Heart"
Linebreak: "Homophone"
Los Angeles Review: "Hornets"
Meridian: "Anecdote of the Swan"
Mid-American Review: "To Be Loved"
New Orleans Review: "Ode to Sneakers"
Pebble Lake Review: "Thought, Barefoot"
The Pinch: "Aubade with Tortoiseshell & Ox," "The Orchard
    Keeper"
Potomac Review: "Scarecrows"
Quarterly West: "Summer in Paradise"
RHINO: "California"
Rougarou: "Portrait of My Mother as Demeter"

Salamander: "Cicadas"

Third Coast: "Postmortem Aubade"

Toad: "Doubting the Gods," "First Harvest"

West Branch: "Self-Portrait as a Butoh Dancer," "Self-Portrait
During a Tornado Sighting"

"Homosexuality" was reprinted in *Best New Poets 2012*. "First Harvest"
was reprinted by *Lambda Literary Review*. "Wilderness of Flesh" will
be reprinted in *Queer Nature* (Autumn House Press, 2021).

This book owes an enormous debt to the people who have supported
me with their kindness, wit, and generosity as I wrote and rewrote it.

To Allison Joseph and Brian Turner, thank you for seeing value in
my work. To the fine folks at Southern Illinois University Press, I
appreciate the tireless effort you put into bringing my book to life.

I am grateful to my teachers, Stephen Yenser, Calvin Bedient, Kathy
Fagan, and Henri Cole, for their many years of patience and guidance.

I am thankful to my former classmates at at Ohio State, Ben Glass,
James Ellenberger, Lo Kwa, Nick McRae, Alex Fabrizio, Matt Sumpter,
Nathan Thomas, and Michael Marberry, for always challenging me and
giving me something to chew on.

Thank you to Allison Davis for sharing your tales of Youngstown,
your Haggadah, and many plates of vegan cookies with me. Thank
you to Nick White for those nights we spent watching *RuPaul's Drag
Race in your tiny apartment*. Matthew Siegel, thank you for the sake
and brownies that winter you took me under your wing in Chicago.
Thank you to Zubair Ahmed for giving me a place to live when I
needed it most. And to Eduardo Corral, I am forever grateful for the
incredible gift of your mentorship.

This book would not be what it is without the keen insights of Jacques
Rancourt, Shelley Wong, and especially Richie Hofmann.

I would also like thank my mother, Mara, and stepfather, Rick, for
their unconditional love and support, and all the sacrifices they made
while raising me.

And finally, to my husband, Trung, thank you for everything.